Beholder

Beholder

Poems by Liz Abrams-Morley

Word Poetry

Published by Word Poetry
P.O. Box 541106
Cincinnati, OH 45254-1106

ISBN: 978-1-62549-271-5

Poetry Editor: Kevin Walzer
Business Editor: Lori Jareo

Visit us on the web at www.wordpoetrybooks.com

Cover art: "The Little Things," Vincent Amicosante © 2017
Cover design by Vincent Amicosante
http://amicosante.com

Author photo: Judy Gelles

Acknowledgments

Some of these poems appeared in these or slightly earlier versions in the following publications to which the author gives abundant thanks:

Houseguest (Liminal; In Case of Attack)

Innisfree Journal (Bird's Eye)

Literary Mama (Sixth Day)

PoemMemoirStory (October's End)

Passager (Miracle)

The author would like to thank *Jewish Currents Magazine*, publishers of the anthology of Raynes Poetry Prize award winners entitled *Urge* (2016) in which "Polishing the Stainless" originally appeared.

"Polishing the Stainless" also appeared online as part of the anthology *All We Can Hold: Poems of Motherhood*, May 2017.

"Deuteronomy, 30:19" appears in the chapbook *Not Our President,* from Moonstone Arts, November, 2017.

The quote in the final stanzas of "Miracle" is from Albert Einstein.

The epigraph is from Ellen Bass, *The Human Line,* "Birdsong from My Patio," 2007, Copper Canyon Press.

A shout out to Tracey Hunt at Winslow's Tavern, Wellfleet, MA for oysters and Sauvignon Blanc and camaraderie at the ends of writing retreat days; many of these poems were created or revised on Wellfleet retreat.

Thanks to my Around the Block Writers' Collaborative partners, Tracy Robert and Sara Kay Rupnik, and to all of our writer participants, muses and fellow travelers.

Thank you hardly seems adequate to my believing mirrors and early readers on much of this work, Tracy Robert and Benay Dara-Abrams, and to my children, Jesse and Erica and their children, Rebecca, Calvin, Sarah and Wesley, who provide the inspiration and impetus to tell the tales and to keep looking—outward and inward.

Special and heartfelt gratitude to Vincent Amicosante for his cover art, and for offering ongoing artist to artist dialogue and inspiration. Please visit Vincent Amicosante at his website, http://amicosante.com, on Facebook, and at the Harmon Gallery, Wellfleet, Massachusetts.

This collection, as is all else, is for Steve.

.... with all that's been ruined
these songs impale the air
with their sharp, insistent needles.

Ellen Bass

Table of Contents

Beholder

Georgia O'Keeffe saw in Manhattan, canyons made of steel. Critics saw flesh in her flowers. What are *labia doing on Grandma's nursing home wall, I ask myself,* my friend Felicia says. Her mother's decorated halls with Georgia's art, posters placed not to titillate but to camouflage institutional green for a woman who'd loved the deep purples and fuchsias of her gone gardens. O'Keeffe said, *I thought I was painting irises, camellias; I thought pears were just pears.* Red sandstone rises above me, skyscrapers to my New York eye on Utah, on Zion.

It's all in the eye.

Deuteronomy, 30:19

After the painting "Everyone Here Speaks Latin"
Max Ernst 1943

Everyone here speaks Latin and when
   birds settle on pin oak and pitch pine:
      song. In the woods, wild turkeys guard
         their nests. There will be young. Hush!

The woodpecker rat-ta-tats at grubs
   under soft gray bark and soon red-rimmed
      leaves will stretch from limbs, unfold into full-
         blown spring which lasts

a day or two here on the Outer Cape, or so
   goes native lore anyway, and summer follows
      close on brief spring's clawed feet. August
         last year, gypsy moths like some

fluttering mushroom cloud enveloped
    oaks and gnawed bare a year's worth of
        foliage in two weeks of tree holocaust.
            Winter iced the hydrangea.

It's easy to dream most nights of other
    mushroom clouds—North Korea, maybe, maybe
        Russia—your grandbabies looking up in awe
            and gone. The madman in the capital

barely speaks English and never in complete
    sentences. Still the ignorant salute while you,
        in your garden, unearth words, Orwell and Atwood,
            as you plant root vegetables and bulbs that will be

next year's bright daffodils and velvety tulips. Choose
    next year. Trim forsythia. Fill a vase to place on your
        table. Fear will flatten you fast as any nightmare's
            spectral blast. Raise your shades. Choose resistance.

Etched in Stone

i.

She plants butterfly bushes, but what
will flutter in? The monarchs are disappearing,
their long flights from Mexico to Pacific Grove,
their sojourns to Cape May— *something about changing currents
or humans fucking with the climate*, her friend Vincent says. He says,

*we all focus on the big things but watch: it'll be
a bunch of little losses that do us in—
bumblebees going, the monarchs.
Things are disappearing,* and she remembers, suddenly,
the autumn of ladybugs: Dorset, Vermont,

her mother felled the brutal winter before.
The ladybugs appeared on the shutters and windows,
door of the rented New England salt box
and the locals, without lifting a brow,
said, *Oh yeah, happens every year. Used to be*

way more of them, while the shingles gleamed—beaded, sequined—
insects clinging to the sunny side of the house. The bugs
lasted maybe two days before moving on though she found stragglers,

a few dried corpses, into November. Crushed,
their brittle wings trailed red dust across pages of failed elegies.

ii.

Monuments planed by rain, names lost to weather.
When did *etched in stone* come to mean *forever?*

iii.

Year's end, she lights a candle for her lost mother, the wick
flickering in slight breath, her window panes unglazed,
the flame a firefly trapped in a jar.

iv.

And fireflies, Vincent's saying, *who sees them anymore?*
A few specimens in shrubs, one or two some nights,
three or four a season, someone inevitably singing out*:*
Look! Lightning bug!

Yeah, he says, *remember when it was just
'oh yeah, lightning bugs. Must be summer.'*

Rebecca Expects Butterflies

i.

We dream little houses.
We dream little houses of sand
on sky, on pinwheels, Lego sets
of little houses, as petals
of a pink flower, black and white
amid red ripe tomatoes.
Rebecca paints houses with little
hands. I collage little houses, glue
them into every landscape because
every landscape needs glue these days.

I am building collage houses
because everywhere now are the sounds
of tearing down.

ii.

Rebecca digs in the sand, unearths
clam halves, presses one to the small
perfect shell of her ear and claims
she can hear the ocean. She gathers
rocks at the breaker line;

I think of David, wonder where,
as she grows, she will sling her stone.

iii.

Each caterpillar she rescues from the wheel
of our car and places back into the woods

will denude another oak.   *You can't hear
the sea in a clam shell,* I won't tell her.

She says she is Wonder Woman.
She expects butterflies.

Already moth holes dot the umbrella
we crank open over the patio table.

Sunlight bullets its not quite shaded surface.
Rebecca sees tiny spirits dancing.

Liminal

Spume at the breaker line neither
sand nor sea, foam mica flecked,
not liquid, not solid.

Crabs, green in storm light,
brown under Florida sun;
this is what the eye does.

Dawn over Captiva Island's Gulf
comes slow, palms inked blue-
black against gray sky,

gradual verdigris
introduced into the scene
and then it's sudden.

Daylight defines beige trunks once
gray, rounds the contours, paints
on the landscape three pink

Adirondack chairs: shadows, outline.
With dawn, they become specific,
bright, reveal on each a plaque inscribed

private, private, private, as if

a word affixed could keep a weary straggler
from resting her feet, could draw a line
between mine and not mine, yours

and not yours. One word, antonym for
the extra cup on every Seder table,
for the door, even in the skeptic's home,

maybe not flung open but left,
every Passover, at least
slightly ajar.

In Case of Attack

Circle the wagons, dive
under your desk, step away
from windows.

None of this advice is ever
good. Once you learned
Dew Line Road was named for

Cold War paranoia— *Distant
Early Warning*—and not droplets,
early summer moisture you'd see

gleaming on dense dune grasses
each morning as you biked past long shuttered
air base housing, a gate off its hinges,

Keep Out sign askew and faded,
the romance was over. Even when you spied
a red fox, her kit trailing her, their tails

auburn flags in May sunrise.
She stopped, froze, the kit too,
froze on cue and stared you down

as if to say: *Try it. Just fucking try it,*
which of course you wouldn't.
I come in peace, you heard yourself say,

stupidly. The rusted chains on swings
half cracked in the playground
of the abandoned air base, creaked,

and you blinked first, averted your gaze
to where a splintering ladder
leaned against a one-story bungalow.

A hazard, you thought, to have it there,
inviting bored kids to climb onto a roof
that's clearly rotting and maybe tumble

into a shattering window, into a kitchen
that could not be torn down, the rumored
cost to do it right too high, the pipes,

all that old asbestos.
And by the time you looked back,
the foxes had made evasive maneuvers,

even their orange bright tails
camouflaged into
the tall green grass.

Bird's Eye

It's an answer to a prayer
never uttered,
the way sun breaks through
as you rise above clouds.

At the airport below, you left
your definition of January:
wind, sleet, snow,
the de-icer blowing

green goo onto wings
turning the plane the bright hue
of pureed spinach,
as when, for so many rote years

you stuffed baby food, homemade,
into small sterilized jars
and moved on auto-pilot
entombed in every bitter season.

How long since you've seen
clouds, really seen them—

this angle, bird's eye, white-backed
below you, bellies, gray and overfed,
facing downward, emptying
out their treacheries: storm or ice.

Or maybe not.
Flying south now, maybe you've
left foul weather behind you;
maybe all clouds are cumulus,

bellies white as their backs,
white as refined sugar, *white
and pale as the driven snow*
first spied on a new land by a planeload--

Sudan's Lost Boys, already thrice displaced,
who had been taught the simile
while scratching lessons into Kenya's
unforgiving baked earth,

but remained naïve about what
awaited them: their promised future,
the part they were never told,
how snow= tactile+ wet+ cold.

Slanted

Because the earth is tilted on its axis
by 23.5 degrees, my neighbor hangs

wind chimes from the sapling branch
of a newly planted tree and I listen

to glass on glass with no breeze blowing.
We will never live in silence, really.

Even stone-deaf as my father became,
he heard the chatter in his head late

into blue-black night, alone in the wide
sea of a bed he kept long after my mother

died unexpectedly early in her strong life.
I'm sure he heard the screech of the rusted

world turning, or at least leaning, alop
on poles he always assumed were upright

as my spine as I sit on my mat,
trying to embrace in my only partly quieted

mind the universality of all things, the hand
that holds the broom fused with the broom

become one with the crumbs on the floor, later,
the face in the mirror merging with the face

of the stranger pumping gas at the next pump,
yoga class over, rain pelting the overhang

at the station. He could be a rearrangement
of genes from the same puddle, I think

then: *he looks like the one*
who did it... here in the neighborhood

where, the morning after November's election,
swastikas appeared spray painted on

deli windows in front of which my son held his
three- year-old, Sarah, awaiting

a bus to carry them to her daycare, his job.
That morning the tilt of the earth must have felt

far more obtuse than 23.5 degrees to him
as he turned the child to face the street

before he'd have to answer questions
he couldn't.   He must have wondered why

the small toaster oven in the lunchroom at work
didn't slide off the counter. Level as it looked,

the world so damned skewed.

Word

> "We flood communities with so many
> guns that it's easier for a teenager to get
> his hands on a glock than...on a computer
> or even a book."
> Barrack Obama, July 12, 2016

Yeah, he says, *I'm the designer, it's all
in the design,* his deconstructed peace sign spells
G-I-V-E across tie-dyed sweatshirts,
*I see you see it, the puzzle, what the word creates,
pieces of peace,* he says, he says *Listen here, I was just listening
to my president, did you hear him on the radio?
down there in Dallas, another funeral I guess he's had practice but
Consoler in chief? The man's got words, I always wanted words—
Yeah, I was an architect, but buildings... I mean,
what do buildings say? I needed to say something solid, you know, the guns,
the news, all those funerals now I say it with shirts.* Proffered
palm turns skyward as if he's asking me to dance, waves across
the span of his craft fair booth to a sweatshirt alive

in oranges and yellows. *You like that one?*
Lady who came just before you wanted
to know couldn't I put the symbols on the back and so not
distract from the colors—showed me her back when I said no
but you got to see a face when you see these words coming
toward you, we need, urgent now, he says *to start*
a conversation, and he's barely taken a breath, but I guess
what he means by conversation is that my eye contact
is enough my nodding when he says *I only make hoodies anymore you*
know why, right? is enough, *hoodies and onesies and toddler tees,*
he says, *never too early to bring the word.*

She Begins

Her dimpled hands pull fat tomatoes—
Not the orange or green,
Two hands! Her mother screams from the kitchen,
a Jack- in- the- Beanstalk vine
behind my son's narrow Philadelphia row.
Fruit jaggedly sliced, chunks of sea salt cracked,
a heavy blue platter carried to a hungry table.
Grandpa, you want the first one?

She awaits the ritual, my husband's familiar hand
forking the proffered piece toward
his mouth, his mouth moving without sound,
she'heheyanu v'kiy'manu v'higi'anu la'z'man
ha'ze, a few words of gratitude for the first of
anything—no moment too small, he'd learned—
his son's first tooth, his daughter's first word
written in wobbly crayon.
Thank you God that I am seeing this day,
incantation learned from his rationalist
German father, over whose seemingly deaf ears

my husband's hands once placed,
ever so gently, headphones, after a stroke took away
his fire, his strength, the cussedness of him, doctors offering
so little; *music maybe?* The old man's hands
became butterflies, swooped before his head,
his own shut eyes,
conducted Ravel, Debussy, Bach, then,
as the last notes sounded, dropped to the mattress.

After, it was his widow's manicured nails, how she picked
lint or brushed dandruff from my stiffening shoulders
when I became her new improvement project.
Still they seemed so fragile in the end,

her palm in mine—the bones twigs, knuckles burls,
the mottled parchment skin of her.
The end came suddenly,
a fall in the night, cracked neck,
one lucid day. Three days before, around
the art museum's floors, she ran, pointing me toward
her world before
Hitler.

See this one? The bold color? Leger.   My mother painted with him.
See that one? Le Corbusier.

Picture this: it's 1928,
Paris comes to Dresden,
my mother-in-law's mother steps
from a cab, enters a shabby studio, removes a glove
finger by finger, easing buttery calf-skin from one hand
with the deft fingers of the other. She steps up
to the blank canvas. She lifts
a brush dabbed in cadmium yellow,
in alizarin crimson.
She begins.

Tracks

A rabbi, a priest and an imam walk into
a bar—or into the road, you think, and see
a semi bearing down.   Some days
you know you're the windshield;
lately you've felt like the bug.

So it goes.

Outside, a turkey crosses the dead end road,
takes his feathered-ass time, head bobbing
as if he's plugged into the '60's oldies you
blast in the car, hands drumming the wheel,
mind skipping tracks every two and a half
minutes, the length of a typical song.

Life's hard

the greeting card on your dresser reads,
get a manicure and a really cute helmet.
You watch out your window, see the turkey's
moving ahead.   Can a dead end be a destination?
You've stumbled on so many of them in your

lifetime but now you find one trail winds into
another and you're willing to

follow.

Map a path to a lake you know, only to pass it,
and your feet lead you to some unnamed
overgrown pond where a great blue heron
rising from a fallen log is your reward for picking
your way down a desire line.

The desire

of others has flattened a narrow strip of foliage
but only slightly. To walk here, place one foot
directly in front of the other as if on a balance beam.
The heron circles the pond, lands on a low branch,
his watery double wavering beneath him, an image
that never quite settles before he

lifts off.

Sixth Day

For Calvin and Erica

His cry sounds the high notes—
oboe or clarinet—this must be what the poets
mean by *reedy,* I say. I say: *Please*
listen carefully as all of your options

have changed.
Radically.

For instance— the neglected hibiscus—offering
without water, a flagrant red-orange blossom.
For awe: Press 1
For exhaustion: Press 2

(Both at once for a chord.)
The flower, the baby—

neither expected so early in the year,
in a February so redolent of spring, magnolias
in their confusion push forth
furred gray buds. But the hibiscus flower

will drop in a day, unlike the baby,
who wakes to nurse every hour.

Your life will never be the same
I want to tell my daughter but she
knows that and anyway—*what life is?*
she'd likely ask, or—*same as what*
anyway?

Polishing the Stainless

i.

I randomly imagine Eve,
first bride before bridal showers, fingering with woe
her flatware—spoons mismatched:
silver, stainless, round-bowled, oblong— scoops for her apple-
sauce with cloves, for the soups made from the array
of vegetables in the garden: butternut squash,
pepper, wax bean, snap pea. *Dig in,*
she'd have said to Adam if he'd let her

have words but he claimed them, left her
to harvest fruits: ok with her. Language alone,
she could have told him, wouldn't nourish
the children who she couldn't even keep
from killing each other.
I once had a friend who stole

ii.

one teaspoon from each café, diner,
dive she ate in, 45 states and a few foreign nations.
In our shared apartment, Madison, 1972, she loved to serve
her legendary soups to our friends, leftovers stewed for hours
over low heat, a beat up stock pot on the avocado stove.
Every place at our cigarette-scarred wooden table was set
with one of her collection.
Dig in! Dig in! She said she stole

because she craved the words, because for each spoon
she knew the story. Later I moved
onto a street of neat, three-bedroom
houses where behind doors, women silently
set tables with floral cloths and matched flatware.
Some had refrigerators magnet-papered in crayoned

families, tempera paint handprints, report cards pocked by
A's and B's—appliances become shrines to the ephemera

of their children's lives . Then babies grew up, cleared out.
Mothers refused to move. What would they do about drawers
filled with old tee shirts, pj's, jeans the kids had left behind
and just might need if they decided to sleep over?

Unused rooms kept swept, beds left made, as if daughters,
as if sons, would slide into deserted spaces at the dinner table,
pick up spoons and resume the conversation,
the way one piece, suddenly retrieved from under the bureau,
slides into emptiness
and completes the jigsaw puzzle.

iii.

After her not-quite-grown son died, my sister cleaned out
the stainless steel refrigerator, turned from hearth to earth,
her new yard on a small pond where no one asked her
to name her sorrow. She suspended spoons,
forks, knives from driftwood, hung these by lengths of dental floss,
created wind chimes which clattered and scared off

crows, red foxes, even coyotes. She ripped into
trim green lawn, planted beans, squash, tomatoes so fat
and sweet they bent vines straight down to dirt.
Love apples someone called them and she loved them,
harvested them gently with scarred bare hands.

Two Children are Threatened by a Nightingale

After the painting by that name by Max Ernst, 1924

I see them, ducking, the way mine ran away from gulls, swooping,
chasing them from breaker line up a September beach, Tashlich, Cape
May: how did we not see this coming? Beaks sharp, squawks piercing
sunlight and a New Year's Day One that nearly ended us, the celestial
book open, our names as yet unrecorded. Pieces of fried dough flying,
caught by what my husband dubbed *those rats of the air* or *pigeons of
the sea,* powdered sugar stuck that night to children's sweatshirts and
jeans, greased paper plates white knuckled in their small hands all that
remained—the damned gulls were the only ones sated. We'd wanted to
cast into the Atlantic one funnel cake and a year's worth of sin, enter
redemption Jewish style before the ledger was blotted and shut tight for
another year. *Do we even believe in a hereafter*—they asked—*in heaven
or hell?*

The older I get, the more I can't tell.

October's End: Eve Returns to the Garden

Feed me red and purple before
my bones dry white.
Feed me the last chirps of birds
before frost, before journeys south.
Feed me the rustle of leaves,

scurry of squirrel feet, acorns
gathered and secreted in oak leaf piles
under trees become skeletal, before snow
blankets the cold earth, before seeds
lie dormant underneath, before growth

seems a forgotten dream. Long ago,
mint tinted languid afternoons.
Now, before dusk, russet daisies rustle,
dun-gold flowers dot the path beside
a muddied pond where

brown-orange carp have grown large
and slow, prepare to lower themselves
further into watery depths and sleep
under a scrim of ice.   Brittle lily stems rise
without flower.   Where petals have dropped

what remains resembles celestial microphones.
How long since these picked up Your signal?
Feed me a signal, any small sign:
a vee of geese India inked across flannel sky,
the scent of green rot's return to earth,

goldenrod's tickle. See how a ladder leans
against gray shingles of the weathered shed's
wall. If I were to climb it,
would I find a woman's dream, find myself naked,
gleaming, my garden fertile?

Everything ends, You lectured as we left,
but you never mentioned the consolation
of endings: how brightly
maple leaves flame before they dry,
before their fall.

Miracle

for Wesley

You make of your mouth a mirror of mine as if,
at 3 months, your own creation story sits on the tip
of the tongue in that toothless cave we call your mouth.

You fill your eyes with bare branches of magnolia,
your ear with the drip of snow melt. Maybe you think you hear
milk flow, sun finally chasing winter from our city stoop.

Take time to look, Georgia O'Keeffe is said to have said.
I once had a teacher who told me, *Don't ever write about your
grandmother. Everyone has a grandmother.*

Nights when I was not much older than you are now,
I watched mine brush the snow river of her hair,
100 strokes root to ends each night, as her glacial blue eyes

stared off somewhere. Maybe she looked back into
azure shadowed woods. Maybe her ear cradled the hollow
beat of hooves, her nose the odor of Cossacks, their approaching

horses. That fool teacher wanted me to write only Cossack poems
when my ear was tuned by the swish of an old woman's brush:

36

Root to end, 100 strokes, my bubby transformed,

become Rapunzel. This was my miracle each evening.
In the morning, she was all tight bun and business.
Now cirrus wisps striate a milk-blue sky and,

for the first time since your birth, the scent of earth screams
spring, even as oil black ice clings to sidewalks.
One day I'll tell you about the burning bush,

how Moses had to stop and look
to see and hear the miracle. Today I point out the first
crocus and your mouth shapes the O of crocus. I tell you

how the hibiscus bush, hauled in from the patio late in fall,
and which just last week I could have sworn I'd killed,
was only sleeping. Now it presses watery green leaves

from dried stalks. Wesley, Look!
it will flower again. Listen: *There are two ways*
to live... as if nothing is a miracle... as if

everything is. Let others live in dark forests,
hoof beats of Cossacks their memories' bass line.
Let them wake each day and call that living.

About the Author

Liz Abrams-Morley's collection, *Inventory*, was published by Finishing Line Press in 2014. *Necessary Turns* was published by Word Poetry in 2010 and won an Eric Hoffer Award for Excellence in Small Press Publishing that year. Her poems and short stories have been published in a variety of nationally distributed anthologies, journals and ezines, and have been read on NPR. She is co-founder of *Around the Block Writing Collaborative* (www.aroundtheblockwriters.org). A professor at Rosemont's MFA program who also teaches children at all levels in literacy in the arts school programs, wife, mother, grandmother and activist, Liz wades knee deep in the flow of everyday life from which she draws inspiration and, occasionally, exasperation.

Visit her at www.lizabramsmorley.org.

93158434R00033

Made in the USA
Columbia, SC
09 April 2018